Australia

OUR ISLAND PARADISE

Australia

OUR ISLAND PARADISE

Photography by *Ken Duncan*

PANOGRAPHS®
PUBLISHING PTY LTD

THIS BOOK IS DEDICATED TO THE LORD GOD ALMIGHTY, CREATOR OF HEAVEN AND EARTH

Special Thanks

It is often said that one picture is worth a thousand words. This can be true but I believe many of those words testify to a variety of other factors that enabled the image to be captured. Without help from the many people and companies around me, it would be difficult for me to follow my dream of photographing the world as I see it. So I would like to say a big thank you to all those who have helped me along the way.

Special thanks to my great staff who can share equal pride in all we have achieved as a team. Thanks also to my family and friends and to all those I have met on my journeys. You have all added character and colour to my life. May you be blessed as you have blessed me.

I would also like to acknowledge the following companies for their assistance.

KEN DUNCAN

As a photographer, it is critical to have a supplier of photographic equipment and consumables that you can trust. The team at L&P is fantastic. They have been invaluable in my transition to the high end digital imaging, supplying my Phase One camera equipment, which I highly recommend.

www.lapfoto.com.au   www.phaseone.com

I have travelled throughout Australia, including many of its most remote locations. When doing this you need the best equipment. There is nothing more trustworthy than ARB gear – from my IPF lights (to show the way) and drawers (that protect my gear) to my Warn winch that hauls me to safety.

www.arb.com.au

Lumix Cameras from Panasonic really put the fun back into photography. I always carry one or more of these wonderful cameras for those spontaneous photo opportunities. The quality is so good that I can even use these images and amazing video footage for professional productions.

www.panasonic.com.au

EPSON
EXCEED YOUR VISION

When it comes to inkjet printing technology Epson is without doubt the market leader. Whether for professional or home applications you can be guaranteed of quality prints that will last. I believe there is no other inkjet process that can come close to the sharpness and colour reproduction of an Epson UltraChrome print.

www.epson.com.au

Josephine Falls, Wooroonooran National Park, Qld

Morning Mystique, Cape Otway, Vic

Contents

Mossman George, Mossman, Qld

Tacking Point Lighthouse, Port Macquarie, NSW

Edeowie Woolshed, Flinders Ranges, SA • *opposite page:* Hopetoun Falls, Otway State Forest, Vic

Brumby Roundup, Benambra, Vic

Uluru, NT • *opposite page:* Ormiston Gorge, West MacDonnell National Park, NT

24   *top:* Sunrise, The Nut, Stanley, Tas • *bottom:* Cape Peron, WA

The distinctive Hebel Hotel was originally opened as a Cobb and Co stopover in 1894. Some years later it began to operate as a hotel and, according to locals, has not changed much since then.

Aussies love a great story and the pub is where you usually hear the tallest tales in town. It may have something to do with the lubricants that one is served in a pub, but the truth can tend to become quite fuzzy.

Hebel is an unpretentious town, but this iconic Aussie pub has a colourful history. Legend has it that Dan Kelly and Steve Hart — members of the infamous "Kelly Gang" — resided for a time in Hebel under assumed identities and drank at this very watering hole. So you never know whom you might meet while having a quiet drink in an authentic Aussie pub.

Early on the morning of 8 June 2007 the bulk carrier *Pasha Bulker* received a warning to move out to sea to escape the approaching storm. Sadly that warning went unheeded. When the storm hit, *Pasha Bulker* was unable to clear the coast and ran aground on Nobbys Beach. The following day a salvage team boarded the ship to assess the condition of the hull and decided to try to refloat the giant vessel. The first two attempts failed and many so-called experts were saying they should give up and just cut the ship up where she lay. But the salvage team didn't give up. On 2 July 2007 they were successful in refloating the ship. I love this shot as it reminds me that even when everyone else says to give up, there is still hope that your dream may float again.

Pebbly Beach, Crescent Head, NSW • *opposite page:* Lighthouse Beach, Seal Rocks, NSW

Sunrise, Wineglass Bay, Tas

Morning Mist, Ellery Creek, NT

Kintore Awakening, Mount Kintore, NT

Birdsville Pub, Birdsville, Qld • *opposite page:* Benambra Pub, Benambra, Vic

Brumby Muster, Benambra, Vic

Ken Connley is one of Australia's great high country cattlemen. In this shot he is flanked on both sides by some of his new generation sidekicks. They are working a mob of wild brumbies that had been caught up in the highlands, and searching for others lost in the shroud of mist on Ken's property. It is early morning and as the golden sunlight penetrates the wafting clouds this magical scene is unveiled before us. I like to think of this photo as a tribute to these hardy Australian heroes, who – tragically – are now being locked out of the high country by urban bureaucrats. We need to preserve this way of life, for it is characters like this – with such strong connection to our land – who give us great strength and hope for our future.

Totally at home in a world of blue-white ice, these Adelie Penguins are a symbol of "Life at the Edge". The realities of the freezing conditions were only too apparent while I was photographing this scene. We'd put out from the ship in a Zodiac inflatable, warned that if we fell into the icy sea we could be dead within two minutes. Floating by this small iceberg, I noticed the lines of cloud radiating from the background and the glowing aqua of the submerged parts of the ice.

I was using my Linhof large-format camera and had to hand-hold the camera while hanging right over the edge of the inflatable to get this shot. How conscious I was of that "two minutes and you're dead!" warning. The name, "Antarctic Raft", is a play on the double meaning of raft – both a group of penguins and a floating platform.

King Penguins, Macquarie Island • *opposite page:* Royal Penguins, Macquarie Island

Ellery Creek, West MacDonnell National Park, NT

Twelve Apostles Sunset, Port Campbell National Park, Vic

Lucky Bay, Cape Le Grand National Park, WA

64 Cape Leeuwin Lighthouse, WA • *opposite page:* Chalahn Falls, Lamington National Park, Qld

Barron Falls, Barron Gorge National Park, Qld • *opposite page:* Bindoola Falls, The Kimberley, WA

Blair's Hut, Alpine National Park, Vic

Corrugated Iron, Outback NSW • *opposite page:* Pebbles, Flynns Beach, Port Macquarie, NSW

Haasts Bluff, NT • *opposite page:* Cedar Falls, Dorrigo National Park, NSW • Ocean River, Hardy's Reef, Qld • Nature's Veil, Beauchamp Falls, Vic

Olgas Sunrise, Kata Tjuta, NT

God's Marbles, Wauchope, NT

Northern Territory

The Northern Territory, where Mick "Crocodile" Dundee became a legend, probably has more intriguing characters than all the other states put together. It has an abundance of interesting Aussies, both male and female, from diverse ethnic backgrounds, including many from the local indigenous population. When these characters start telling colourful yarns of their outback adventures, they never allow the truth to get in the way of a good story. They especially love to stir up the tourists with their crocodile stories; there are even stories of people putting crocodiles in someone's backyard swimming pool. After listening to some of these tales, many cautious travellers are not sure if anywhere is safe to swim. The reality is that crocodiles do not constitute a major threat and there are plenty of safe places to swim. It is just the nature of many fun-loving Territorians to want to have a joke with people, but if you needed help they would give you the shirt off their back.

One thing that saddens me about the Northern Territory is that because it is run by the Federal Government, it is one of the most over-regulated parts of Australia. There are many amazing places that the average person is no longer allowed to visit. I'm amazed that the resilient locals have allowed so many of their freedoms to be eroded by over-zealous bureaucrats and politicians. I am sure in time the locals will fight back, as they will only tolerate so much. Maybe they should take a few crocodiles to Canberra and let them loose in some politicians' swimming pools?

Years ago places like Uluru and Kata Tjuta National Park and Kakadu National Park used to be fantastic places to go. Now, with the many restrictions and great loss of freedom, people often refer to these areas as Ulurules and Kakadon't respectively. These are still important places to visit and hopefully, in time, policy makers will understand the great significance of allowing all people to have a connection to the land — not just a select few.

God's Marbles, Wauchope, NT

This place is referred to on maps as "The Devils Marbles" which I think is a ridiculous name for something so beautiful. What has the devil ever done to give him credit for such an artistic site? So I am working to get the name changed to "God's Marbles", which I believe is far more appropriate.

Photo Tip

The hardest part of photography is actually getting out of bed. When you master this, then you're on your way to getting some great opportunities. Early in the morning, there are also less people around to get in the way of your photographs.

Banjo Paterson's famous poem "The Man from Snowy River" really epitomises the spirit of the high country cattlemen of old. Most Australians love this poem because it is the story of an ordinary bloke who pushes hard and overcomes extraordinary odds to achieve the goal – and that pretty much sums up our national character.

Guy's Hut was built in 1940 by Jack Guy to shelter stockmen bringing cattle to the high plains for summer grazing. The stockmen described in Banjo Paterson's poem were the early pioneers of much of our high country regions. They often took shelter in huts like this, many of which are still standing today.

These hardy cowboys continue to overcome everything nature throws at them, but now they have a new battle on their hands – bureaucrats are trying to deny them access to the high country areas. My money is still on "The Man from Snowy River".

People from many different nations have come to call Australia home. The diversity of various nationalities has helped cultivate a multi-layered cultural fabric that makes our nation even stronger.

All around the world people hear of Australia, the world's largest island – a land of freedom, space and opportunity – which is why many try to find a way to come here.

Some have been so desperate to seek a better lifestyle or flee their own war-torn country they are willing to risk their lives crossing the ocean in dubious vessels such as this to reach our island paradise.

Real Aussies don't mind where people come from, so long as when they arrive here they are willing to embrace our nation as their new home. For Australia is a land of opportunity where it is not who you are, but what you're willing to bring to the party, that matters most.

Cockpit Waterfall, Norfolk Island • *opposite page:* Long Jetty, Central Coast, NSW

Trailer Sailor, Morgan, SA • *opposite page:* High Cliff, SA

Kimberley Boabs, The Kimberley, WA

top: Canal Rocks, WA • *bottom:* Whitehaven Beach, Whitsunday Island, Qld

Russell Falls, Mount Field National Park, Tas

Camels, Cable Beach, WA • *opposite page:* Palm Cove, Qld • Tread Lightly, Omeo, Vic • Secret Sanctuary, The Kimberley, WA

Arkaba Woolshed, Flinders Ranges, SA

Little Beach, Two Peoples Bay Nature Reserve, WA

Tulips, Wynyard, Tas

Cephissus Creek, Cradle Mountain – Lake St Clair National Park, Tas • *opposite page:* Cradle Mountain, Cradle Mountain – Lake St Clair National Park, Tas

Brumby Dawn, Benambra, Vic

Weeping Willow, Yarra Valley, Vic

The Crossing, Swift's Creek, Vic

One of the mistakes people make when photographing waterfalls is to get too close. I have made this mistake myself at these very falls. So, on this visit, I determined to capture the essence of the whole location. I climbed up onto a rock ledge to get a wide view, but this is a very popular location and other visitors kept walking into my shot. There seemed a never-ending stream of people! I passed the time by looking at the details in the landscape. The central rock in the mid-ground looks to me like a breaching whale with its mouth open. Finally, at last light, everyone else left. Then, when I thought the curtain on the day was to be drawn closed, there was a surge of beautiful final afterglow light. What a blessing to be the only one there to record this moment of grandeur in the Grampians.

In the dry season, Mitchell Falls is simply a series of five neat, tiered cascades – a tranquil spot, perfect for exploring and a refreshing swim. But after the wet season, as in this shot, the watercourse becomes a raging torrent. Individual tiers are lost in the thundering flow and the water becomes a massive blur of movement. To try swimming at this time of year would possibly be the last of your worst ideas. It is impossible to access the falls by land during or immediately after the wet. A helicopter dropped me in to get this shot, and I marvelled at the raw power of the flood below me. This is nature at its most primeval, a scene that evoked a sense of the very beginning of time.

120   Glycosmis Falls, The Kimberley, WA

Mawson's Hut (detail), Antarctica • *opposite page:* Whitsunday Aerial, Hill Inlet, Qld

Aerial, Whitsunday Island, Qld

top: Island Arch, Port Campbell National Park, Vic • *bottom:* Sunset, Eucla Dunes, WA

Seven Mile Beach, Coffin Bay National Park, SA • *opposite page:* Point Lowly Lighthouse, via Whyalla, SA

Aboriginal Kids, Arnhem Land, NT • *opposite page:* Sunset, Kata Tjuta, NT

Norah Head Lighthouse, NSW

New South Wales

Our indigenous Australians seemed to be doing just fine back in the eightenth century, living in a land of plenty where hundreds of different tribal groups had learned to survive in relative harmony. Of course they had their issues. There were arguments over territories, even some fighting with spears and clubs, but generally they worked out their own problems. Their impact on the environment was minimal and they could have continued on for millennia without causing damage to the land they called home.

In the 1700's strange canoes with large white billowing wind catchers began to arrive from across the seas. These leviathan craft carried ghostly looking creatures in strange plumage, who came ashore. The indigenous people watched as they stuck a flag in the sand and said something about claiming the land for their king. Then in 1788 a large number of those floating things arrived with a big mob of white fellas who stayed and began building dwellings, rushing around like honey ants, sucking the nectar out of everything they could find.

Such were the European beginnings of New South Wales where today over a third of Australia's population lives. Much has changed in the last 200 years or so, but Sydney Cove, where the new colony began, is still unquestionably one of the most beautiful sea ports in the world. The natural harbour and its adjoining waterways form a magnificent foundation on which the jewel of Sydney has been created. Almost everyone has heard of Sydney, if only for its massive New Years fireworks displays, which are televised to millions of people around the world. Just like its fireworks, Sydney is an explosive city bubbling with life, and offers a kaleidoscope of opportunities due to its now diverse multicultural population.

The state of New South Wales is like a sampler of Australia's best offerings. It has everything from outback landscapes and snow-capped mountains (Mount Kosciusko, our highest mountain, is situated in New South Wales) to verdant rainforests, beaches of all shapes and sizes and many interesting coastal features. Some of the must-see regions are the Central Coast (the area I call home), the Blue Mountains, the New England area and the south coast. There's plenty of fun to be had in New South Wales, so I hope to see you in my home state.

Norah Head Lighthouse, NSW

This is one of my favourite spots on the New South Wales Central Coast. I worked on this shot for two weeks before capturing the right conditions.

Photo Tip

Magical photos may take many visits or patience to wait for the right conditions. Don't give up, as stunning images are the reward.

142   Cradle Mountain from Kathleen's Pool, Tas

King George Falls, The Kimberley, WA

Piccaninny Creek, Purnululu National Park, WA • *opposite page:* Boab Tree, Fitzroy Crossing, WA

Ragged Ranges, The Kimberley, WA • *opposite page:* Mertens Falls, The Kimberley, WA

Paradise, Fantome Island, Qld

Sunrise, Main Beach, South West Rocks, NSW

Sunrise, Emily Bay, Norfolk Island

Hill Inlet, Whitsunday Island, Qld

Queensland

Queensland, our "fun in the sun" state, boasts many magnificent places to visit. Their state slogan used to be "beautiful one day and perfect the next", which was often true. But more recently they have moved away from that overly optimistic statement, as our north-eastern state does experience some very wild weather from time to time.

Queenslanders are strong, adaptable people, fiercely proud of their sunshine state. They love their sport and I just wish they didn't play Rugby League so well, as they keep giving us New South Welshmen a hiding (but we haven't given up yet).

Two of my favourite regions of Queensland are the hinterland beyond the capital city of Brisbane and the tropical rainforests and coastal areas near Mossman in the far north of the state. I also enjoy spending time in the outback areas, where there is a profusion of unique Aussie characters including some real rough diamonds that have no trouble keeping city slickers grounded.

For tropical delight nothing beats the Great Barrier Reef and the Whitsunday Island area. There's such a profusion of life and colour in these places: sparkling sunshine, vast blue seas, the marbled patterns of the reef and endless beaches. Here and there you spot the white sails of a lone yacht, heading from one paradise to another. And wherever the land rises above the sand, there's a burst of tropical vegetation, with its cool greens and mottled shadows. If you can't take good photos in such areas, perhaps it's time to give up photography.

Hill Inlet, Whitsunday Island, Qld

What could be more relaxing than spending a day of fun in the sun at one of the world's most beautiful beaches. To me this is like paradise – soaking up the sun, frolicking in the crystal clear water and exploring the island's abundant natural treasures. It doesn't get much better than this.

The sand on this beach is almost pure silica; as white as sand can be. It is so highly reflective that you need to be very diligent in applying sunscreen to every part of your body – even underneath loose-fitting clothing – to avoid sunburn in very sensitive areas. Sunglasses are also a necessity to help combat the glare.

Probably one of the best ways to enjoy this region is by boat. You can bring your own, hire one, or take one of the many day tours on offer. Be sure to pack a cooler with plenty of cold drinks and take a lavish picnic spread to share with your friends. If you're still feeling stressed after a relaxing day in this playground, then maybe it's time for some therapy.

I find that nature has a wonderful ability to wash away the cares of the world, which can hang like a heavy cloak upon us. Relaxing in the sun is – quite simply – good for the soul.

Photo Tip

Sand and salt water are your camera's worst enemies. Always use a dry sack to keep your camera gear in when you are on the beach or out and about on the water in open boats.

Camera Information

Having good equipment really helps you capture images quicker and to a higher technical standard. But gear alone will not guarantee stunning images. I believe the real key to getting great photos is seeing the picture that is there for you to capture. Photos are gifts that we borrow to let others share in our journey. Show me someone's photos and I'll show you the person. It doesn't matter whether you shoot digital or on film, so long as you get the shot. I shoot both, as each has its strengths and a particular feel.

People often ask me about my equipment so I've listed here some of the cameras I currently use.

PHASE ONE 645DF CAMERA

Body with a P65+ back – nicknamed **"Bruce"** after my friend who sold me the camera.

The P65+ back I have is 60 megapixels as I need the biggest possible file size for large prints. The benefit of bigger files is you don't have to stitch images together in order to produce large prints. Bruce allows me to get a big image in one decisive moment. The P65+ back allows 12 f-stops latitude between highlights and shadow, so you can get shots you could never hold together on film (which only allows 4 f-stops of latitude). The Phase One camera also comes with raw converter software called Capture One, which is great for preparing images for different needs.

If you like to know in the field whether you have the shot in the bag, then this is the camera for you.

Shooting wildlife or action with a camera like this will really sort out the weekend warriors from battle-trained pros, as it can be critical in focus and slower to use than traditional 35mm format digital cameras. But when you nail it on this baby you will have a real winner that sets you apart.

Lenses I have for this body are 35mm, 55mm, 80mm, 150mm and, for wildlife, a 500mm.

HORSEMAN SW-D II PRO

– nicknamed **"Horse"** for obvious reasons.

This is the perfect wide angle solution for the Phase One P65+ high-end digital back (the same removable back I use on the P645 camera). If required, you can even attach a film back. Horse has no electronics and no mirrors like SLR-style cameras. It is a viewfinder-style camera: purely an interface between a shuttered lens attached at the front and the digital (or film) back at the rear. Horse's body is machined to very high precision allowing for fine perspective adjustments. With this camera you don't have problems with shake caused by mirror vibrations on exposures. It allows for shift if the lens has enough coverage to allow for movement. For this camera I only have a 23mm Rodenstock HR Digaron lens, which is so wide it just covers the full 6cm x 4.5cm sensor and doesn't allow for any shift. Lenses 35mm and longer do allow for shift. The digital series of lenses from Schneider and Rodenstock designed especially for these cameras are so sharp you may need to carry a box of Bandaids.

LINHOF 617S II CAMERA SYSTEM
– nicknamed simply *"the Hof"*.

These cameras are the "Rolls Royce" of 6cm x 17cm film cameras. The Hof shoots 120 and 220 roll film. It is a viewfinder style of camera with a reasonably accurate viewfinder. I have a special red camera so obviously it goes faster. Linhof camera gear is German engineering and optical craftsmanship at its best, with no batteries needed. For super large panoramic prints, it is still hard to beat the quality of film unless stitching on Phase One. Film and digital really should not be compared as they have a totally different feel. The file size I get when my 6cm x 17cm transparencies are scanned is about 600MB – a lot bigger than any non-scanning digital camera on the market currently.

I still enjoy shooting film, as I love the surprise factor. When you come home and your work is processed, it's so exciting to see the finished results. Some people say they like to shoot digital to save on the cost of film and processing. They tend to forget about the cost of all the computer software and hardware updates and upgrades and the addiction to ever-increasing terabytes of storage space. Storage is an ongoing cost as hardware needs to be upgraded every three to four years.

Linhof uses hand-picked Schneider lenses. They are mind blowing when it comes to sharpness and quality.

Again the shutters are in the lens so there's no camera shake from mirrors in the camera body.

The lenses I use are a 72mm with a centre-weighted filter to compensate for light drop off, a 90mm without any centre-weighted filter and a 180mm without any filtration.

SEITZ ROUNDSHOT 220 VR STANDARD OR 3-D CAMERA SYSTEM — nicknamed *"Johnny 5"*
because in the stereo setup it looks like the robot "Johnny Five" from the movie "Short Circuit"

This camera uses 120 and 220 roll film and is a scanning camera system. Johnny 5 must always be used on a tripod. It gets extremely wide angle shots by rotating the camera and lens from its motorised control base which is in sync with the film moving in the camera. This is a cool, high-tech camera. It takes a little getting used to, but it can capture amazing shots. The camera can be set up to shoot 3-D with two matched cameras or 2-D with only one camera. There are only a couple of these 3-D cameras in the world. You can set the shooting angle to any width you desire. You can even shoot more than 360 degrees so you can be in the image

twice. I normally like to shoot about 230 degrees on a 75mm lens. This gives me a height to width ratio of 1:5 – 6cm high x 30cm long – a serious piece of film.

Johnny 5 allows you to get wide shots with movement, unlike stitching on traditional cameras, which have problems with movement such as waves. You can also set vertical shift on your lenses to position your horizon at the desired level. When Johnny 5 is set up, people just don't have a clue what it is. This is a fun camera.

The lenses I have chosen are Pentax SMC 67 lenses in 45mm, 55mm and 75mm.

LUMIX CAMERAS
Panasonic Lumix LX5 Camera – nicknamed *"Ridiculous"* because it takes great shots so effortlessly that when I look at the results I often say, "that's ridiculous!". This little camera can take such good shots, it's hardly fair.

When it comes to capturing really high quality stills or movie footage with ease (on my adventures or for personal shots) I use Ridiculous. I always carry this wonderfully compact camera and sometimes its big brother, my GH2 Lumix. This camera I call *"Beyond"* because the results I get with this are beyond ridiculous in quality. These latest Lumix cameras are so easy to use that if you can't take great shots with these cameras you should give up photography. Both these cameras shoot in RAW format, which gives greater results.

Photographer's Notes

Front Cover Paradise, Fantome Island, Qld
Camera: Linhof 617S II; Lens: Schneider 90mm; Filters: none; Medium: film, Fuji 120 Velvia 50 ISO; Shutter Speed: 1/8; Aperture: f22.5; Ratio: 3:1; Degrees: 87, shot on tripod; Image Size: 6cm x 17cm

Page 1 Cape Leveque, WA
Camera: Phase One P645 body with P65+ back; 35mm; ISO: 100; Shutter Speed: 1/250; Aperture: f14; Exposure Compensation: 0.0; Resolution: 60.5MP

Pages 2–3 Palm Cove, Cairns, Qld
Camera: Horseman SW-D II Pro body with P45+ back; Lens: 24mm; ISO: 50; Shutter Speed: 1 second; Aperture: f8; Exposure Compensation: 0.0; Resolution: 39MP

Page 5 Red Centre Dreaming, Uluru, NT
Camera: Phase One P645 body with P65+ back; Lens: 35mm; ISO: 50; Shutter Speed: 3 seconds; Aperture: f16; Exposure Compensation: –0.3 Resolution: 60.5MP

Pages 6–7 Josephine Falls, Wooroonooran National Park, Qld
Camera: Phase One P645 body with P45+ back; Lens: 80mm; ISO: 50; Shutter Speed: 1/10; Aperture: f8; Exposure Compensation: 0.0; Resolution: 39MP, 8 image stitch

Page 8 Morning Mystique, Cape Otway, Vic
Camera: Phase One P645 body with P65+ back; Lens: 150mm; ISO: 50; Shutter Speed: 1.3 seconds; Aperture: f16; Exposure Compensation: –0.3; Resolution: 60.5MP

Pages 10–12 Mossman Gorge, Mossman, Qld
Camera: Seitz Roundshot 220 VR; Lens: 55mm Pentax 67 with lens shift; Filters: none; Medium: film, Fuji 220 Velvia 100 ISO; Shutter Speed: 1/4; Aperture: f11; Ratio: 5:1; Degrees: 300, shot on tripod; Image Size: 6cm x 30cm

Page 14 Bird River, Tas
Camera: Horseman SW-D II Pro body with P45+ back; Lens: 24mm; ISO: 50; Shutter Speed: 1 second; Aperture: f11; Exposure Compensation: 0.0; Resolution: 39MP

Page 15 Hidden Treasure, Hamersley Gorge National Park, WA
Camera: Linhof 617S II; Lens: Schneider 72mm; Filters: centre graduating filter; Medium: film, Fuji 220 Velvia 50 ISO; Shutter Speed: 2–4 seconds; Aperture: f32; Ratio: 3:1; Degrees: 100, shot on tripod; Image Size: 6cm x 17cm

Page 15 Emerald Waters, Karijini National Park, WA
Camera: Linhof 617S II; Lens: Schneider 72mm; Filters: centre graduating filter; Medium: film, Fuji 220 Velvia 50 ISO; Shutter Speed: 1–2 seconds; Aperture: f32; Ratio: 3:1; Degrees: 100, shot on tripod; Image size: 6cm x 17cm

Page 15 Journey to the Centre, Karijini National Park, WA
Camera: Linhof 617S II; Lens: Schneider 72mm; Filters: centre graduating filter; Medium: film, Fuji 220 Velvia 50 ISO; Shutter Speed: 2–4 seconds; Aperture: f32; Ratio: 3:1; Degrees: 100, shot on tripod; Image size: 6cm x 17cm

Pages 16–17 Tacking Point Lighthouse, Port Macquarie, NSW
Camera: Linhof 617S II; Lens: Schneider 72mm; Filters: centre graduating filter; Medium: film, Fuji 220 Velvia 100 ISO; Shutter Speed: 15 seconds; Aperture: f22; Ratio: 3:1; Degrees: 100, shot on tripod; Image size: 6cm x 17cm

Page 18 Edeowie Woolshed, Flinders Ranges, SA
Camera: Horseman SW-D II Pro body with P65+ back; Lens: 23mm; ISO: 100; Shutter Speed: 1/4; Aperture: f11; Exposure Compensation: 0.0; Resolution: 60.5MP

Page 19 Hopetoun Falls, Otway State Forest, Vic
Camera: Phase One P645 body with P65+ back; Lens: 35mm; ISO: 50; Shutter Speed: 7/10; Aperture: f16; Exposure Compensation: –2.0; Resolution: 60.5MP

Pages 20–21 Brumby Roundup, Benambra, Vic
Camera: Phase One P645 body with P65+ back; Lens: 150mm; ISO: 200; Shutter Speed: 1/90; Aperture: f4; Exposure Compensation: +0.3; Resolution: 60.5MP

Page 22 Uluru, NT
Camera: Phase One P645 body with P65+ back; Lens: 35mm; ISO: 50; Shutter Speed: 1/160; Aperture: f9; Exposure Compensation: –0.3; Resolution: 60.5MP

Page 23 Ormiston Gorge, West MacDonnell National Park, NT
Camera: Phase One P645 body with P65+ back; Lens: 55mm; ISO: 50; Shutter Speed: 10 seconds; Aperture: f18; Exposure Compensation: 0.0; Resolution: 60.5MP

Pages 24–25 Sunrise, The Nut, Stanley, Tas
Camera: Seitz Roundshot 220 VR; Lens: 75mm Pentax 67 with lens shift; Filters: none; Medium: film, Fuji 220 Velvia 100 ISO; Shutter Speed: 1/2; Aperture: f16; Ratio: 5:1; Degrees: 230, shot on tripod; Image Size: 6cm x 30cm

Pages 24–25 Cape Peron, WA
Camera: Seitz Roundshot 220 VR; Lens: 75mm Pentax 67 with lens shift; Filters: none; Medium: Film, Fuji 220 Velvia 100 ISO; Shutter Speed: 1/4; Aperture: f11; Ratio: 5:1; Degrees: 230, shot on tripod; Image Size: 6cm x 30cm

Pages 26–27 Hebel Hotel, Hebel, Qld
Camera: Horseman SW-D II Pro body with P65+ back; Lens: 23mm; ISO: 50; Shutter Speed: 2 seconds; Aperture: f11; Exposure Compensation: 0.0; Resolution: 60.5MP

Pages 28–29 Pasha Bulker Stranded, Nobbys Beach, NSW
Camera: Linhof 617S II; Lens: Schneider 90mm; Filters: none; Medium: film, Fuji 220 Velvia 100 ISO; Shutter Speed: 4 seconds; Aperture: f22; Ratio: 3:1; Degrees: 87, shot on tripod; Image Size: 6cm x 17cm

Page 30 Pebbly Beach, Crescent Head, NSW
Camera: Horseman SW-D II Pro body with P65+ back; Lens: 23mm; ISO: 50; Shutter Speed: 20 seconds; Aperture: f11; Exposure Compensation: 0.0; Resolution: 60.5MP

Page 31 Lighthouse Beach, Seal Rocks, NSW
Camera: Horseman SW-D II Pro body with P65+ back; Lens: 23mm; ISO: 100; Shutter Speed: 2 seconds; Aperture: f11; Exposure Compensation: 0.0; Resolution: 60.5MP

Pages 32–34 Sunrise, Wineglass Bay, Tas
Camera: Seitz Roundshot 220 VR; Lens: 75mm Pentax 67 with lens shift; Filters: none; Medium: film, Fuji 220 Velvia 100 ISO; Shutter Speed: 1/8; Aperture: f11; Ratio: 5:1; Degrees: 230, shot on tripod; Image Size: 6cm x 30cm

Page 36 Robot, Mutonia Sculpture Park, SA
Camera: Phase One P645 body with P65+ back; Lens: 35mm; ISO: 50; Shutter Speed: 1/60; Aperture: f11; Exposure Compensation: –0.3; Resolution: 60.5MP

Page 37 Flower, Mutonia Sculpture Park, SA
Camera: Phase One P645 body with P65+ back; Lens: 80mm; ISO: 50; Shutter Speed: 1/125; Aperture: f11; Exposure Compensation: –0.3 Resolution: 60.5MP

Page 38 Cable Beach, WA
Camera: Phase One P645 body with P65+ back; Lens: 35mm; ISO: 100; Shutter Speed: 1/15; Aperture: f8; Exposure Compensation: 0.0; Resolution: 60.5MP

Page 39 Sunrise, Norah Head Lighthouse, NSW
Camera: Linhof 617S II; Lens: Schneider 72mm; Filters: centre graduating filter; Medium: film, Fuji 220 Velvia 100 ISO; Shutter Speed: 20 seconds; Aperture: f32; Ratio: 3:1; Degrees: 100, shot on tripod; Image Size: 6cm x 17cm

Page 39 Ellinjaa Falls, Atherton Tablelands, Qld
Camera: Linhof 617S II; Lens: Schneider 90mm; Filters: none; Medium: film, Fuji 220 Velvia 100 ISO; Shutter Speed: 2 seconds; Aperture: f32; Ratio: 3:1; Degrees: 87, shot on tripod; Image Size: 6cm x 17cm

Page 39 Sunrise, The Skillion, Terrigal, NSW
Camera: Linhof 617S II; Lens: Schneider 72mm; Filters: centre graduating filter; Medium: film, Fuji 220 Velvia 100 ISO; Shutter Speed: 30 seconds; Aperture: f32; Ratio: 3:1; Degrees: 100, shot on tripod; Image Size: 6cm x 17cm

Pages 40–41 Morning Mist, Ellery Creek, NT
Camera: Phase One P645 body with P65+ back; Lens: 80mm; ISO: 100; Shutter Speed: 1.6 seconds; Aperture: f20; Exposure Compensation: –0.7; Resolution: 60.5MP, 9 image stitch

Pages 42–43 Kintore Awakening, Mount Kintore, NT
Camera: Linhof 617S II; Lens: Schneider 72mm; Filters: centre graduating filter; Medium: film, Fuji 220 Velvia 100 ISO; Shutter Speed: 1/4; Aperture: f22; Ratio: 3:1; Degrees: 100, shot on tripod; Image Size: 6cm x 17cm

Page 44 Birdsville Pub, Birdsville, Qld
Camera: Horseman SW-D II Pro body with P45+ back; Lens: 24mm; ISO: 100; Shutter Speed: 4 seconds; Aperture: f8; Exposure Compensation: 0.0; Resolution: 39MP

Page 45 Benambra Pub, Benambra, Vic
Camera: Horseman SW-D II Pro body with P65+ back; Lens: 23mm; ISO: 100; Shutter Speed: 3 seconds; Aperture: f11; Exposure Compensation: 0.0; Resolution: 60.5MP

Pages 46–47 Brumby Muster, Benambra, Vic
Camera: Linhof 617S II; Lens: Schneider 90mm; Filters: none; Medium: film, Fuji 220 Velvia 100 ISO; Shutter Speed: 1/8; Aperture: f22; Ratio: 3:1; Degrees: 87, shot on tripod; Image Size: 6cm x 17cm

Pages 48–49 Antarctic Raft, Antarctica
Camera: Phase One P645 body with P45+ back; Lens: 80mm; ISO: 100; Shutter Speed: 1/1250; Aperture: f8; Exposure Compensation: –0.3; Resolution: 39MP

Page 50 King Penguins, Macquarie Island
Camera: Phase One P645 body with P45+ back; Lens: 35mm; ISO: 100; Shutter Speed: 1/80; Aperture: f8; Exposure Compensation: –1.3; Resolution: 39MP

Page 51 Royal Penguins, Macquarie Island
Camera: Phase One P645 body with P45+ back; Lens: 35mm; ISO: 100; Shutter Speed: 1/100; Aperture: f6.3; Exposure Compensation: –0.7; Resolution: 39MP

Pages 52–53 Ellery Creek, West MacDonnell National Park, NT
Camera: Phase One P645 body with P65+ back; Lens: 80mm; ISO: 50; Shutter Speed: 1/4; Aperture: f11; Exposure Compensation: 0.0; Resolution: 60.5MP, 10 image stitch

Pages 54–56 Twelve Apostles Sunset, Port Campbell National Park, Vic
Camera: Seitz Roundshot 220 VR; Lens: 75mm Pentax 67 with lens shift; Filters: none; Medium: film, Fuji 220 Velvia 100 ISO; Shutter Speed: 1 second; Aperture: f11; Ratio: 5:1; Degrees: 240 scan, shot on tripod; Image Size: 6cm x 30cm

Page 58 Ellery Creek Reflections, West MacDonnell National Park, NT
Camera: Phase One P645 body with P65+ back; Lens: 80mm; ISO: 50; Shutter Speed: 8/10; Aperture: f16; Exposure Compensation: 0.0; Resolution: 60.5MP

Page 59 Outback Splendour, West MacDonnell National Park, NT
Camera: Phase One P645 body with P65+ back; Lens: 150mm; ISO: 50; Shutter Speed: 2 seconds; Aperture: f16; Exposure Compensation: –2.0; Resolution: 60MP

Pages 60–61 Lucky Bay, Cape Le Grand National Park, WA
Camera: Linhof 617S II; Lens: Schneider 90mm; Filters: none; Medium: film, Fuji 220 Velvia 100 ISO; Shutter Speed: 1/8; Aperture: f22; Ratio: 3:1; Degrees: 87, shot on tripod; Image Size: 6cm x 17cm

Pages 62–63 A New Day, Wamberal Beach, NSW
Camera: Linhof 617S II; Lens: Schneider 90mm; Filters: 81A; Medium: film, Fuji 120 Velvia 50 ISO; Shutter Speed: 1/2; Aperture: f22; Ratio: 3:1; Degrees: 87, shot on tripod; Image Size: 6cm x 17cm

Page 64 Cape Leeuwin Lighthouse, WA
Camera: Horseman SW-D II Pro body with P65+ back; Lens: 23mm; ISO: 50; Shutter Speed: 16 seconds; Aperture: f11; Exposure Compensation: 0.0; Resolution: 60.5MP

Page 65 Chalahn Falls, Lamington National Park, Qld
Camera: Horseman SW-D II Pro body with P65+ back; Lens: 23mm; ISO: 50; Shutter Speed: 1 second; Aperture: f11; Exposure Compensation: 0.0; Resolution: 60.5MP

Page 66 Barron Falls, Barron Gorge National Park, Qld
Camera: Phase One P645 body with P45+ back; Lens: 35mm; ISO: 50; Shutter Speed: 1/25; Aperture: f12; Exposure Compensation: 0.0; Resolution: 39MP

Page 67 Bindoola Falls, The Kimberley, WA
Camera: Phase One P645 body with P65+ back; Lens: 28mm; ISO: 100; Shutter Speed: 1.6 seconds; Aperture: f8; Exposure Compensation: 0.0; Resolution: 60.5MP

Pages 68–69 Blair's Hut, Alpine National Park, Vic
Camera: Phase One P645 body with P65+ back; Lens: 35mm; ISO: 50; Shutter Speed: 4 seconds; Aperture: f11; Exposure Compensation: –0.3; Resolution: 60.5MP, 10 image stitch

Page 70 Corrugated Iron, Outback NSW
Camera: Phase One P645 body with P65+ back; Lens: 55mm; ISO 50; Shutter Speed: 1/20; Aperture: f16; Exposure Compensation: 0.0; Resolution: 60.5MP

Page 71 Pebbles, Flynns Beach, Port Macquarie, NSW
Camera: Phase One P645 body with P65+ back; Lens: 80mm; ISO 100; Shutter Speed: 6/10; Aperture: f22; Exposure Compensation: 0.0; Resolution: 60.5MP

Page 72 Haasts Bluff, NT
Camera: Phase One P645 body with P45+ back Lens: 35mm; ISO: 50; Shutter Speed: 1/6; Aperture: f10; Exposure Compensation: –0.3; Resolution: 39MP

Page 73 Cedar Falls, Dorrigo National Park, NSW
Camera: Linhof 617S II; Lens: Schneider 90mm; Filters: none; Medium: film, Fuji 220 Velvia 100 ISO; Shutter Speed: 1 second; Aperture: f22; Ratio: 3:1; Degrees: 87, shot on tripod; Image Size: 6cm x 17cm

Page 73 Ocean River, Hardy's Reef, Qld
Camera: Linhof 617S II; Lens: Schneider 90mm; Filters: none; Medium: film, Fuji 220 Velvia 100 ISO; Shutter Speed: 1/250; Aperture: f11; Ratio: 3:1; Degrees: 87, handheld; Image Size: 6cm x 17cm

Page 73 Nature's Veil, Beauchamp Falls, Vic
Camera: Linhof 617S II; Lens: Schneider 72mm; Filters: centre graduating filter; Medium: film, Fuji 220 Velvia 100 ISO; Shutter Speed: 8 seconds; Aperture: f22; Ratio: 3:1; Degrees: 100, shot on tripod; Image Size: 6cm x 17cm

Pages 74–75 Olgas Sunrise, Kata Tjuta, NT
Camera: Phase One P645 body with P65+ back; Lens: 80mm; ISO: 50; Shutter Speed: 1/15; Aperture: f14; Exposure Compensation: 0.0; Resolution: 60.5MP, 9 image stitch

Pages 76–78 God's Marbles, NT
Camera: Seitz Roundshot 220 VR; Lens: 75mm Pentax 67 with lens shift; Filters: none; Medium: film, Fuji 220 Velvia 50 ISO; Shutter Speed: 1/4; Aperture: f11; Ratio: 5:1; Degrees: 225 scan, shot on tripod; Image Size: 6cm x 30cm

Page 80 Glenworth, Central Coast, NSW
Camera: Canon EOS 5D Mark II; Lens: 24–70mm @ 24mm; ISO: 1000; Shutter Speed: 1/250; Aperture: f2.8; Exposure Compensation: +0.3; Resolution: 21.2MP

Page 81 Autumn Leaves, Central Coast, NSW
Camera: Horseman SW-D II Pro body with P65+ back; Lens: 23mm; ISO: 100; Shutter Speed: 1/4; Aperture: f11; Exposure Compensation: 0.0; Resolution: 60.5MP

Pages 82–83 Guy's Hut, Alpine National Park, Vic
Camera: Linhof 617S II; Lens: Schneider 90mm; Filters: none; Medium: film, Fuji 220 Velvia 50 ISO; Shutter Speed: 1/4; Aperture: f22; Ratio: 3:1; Degrees: 87, shot on tripod; Image Size: 6cm x 17cm

Pages 84–85 Abandoned Boat, Willies Creek, WA
Camera: Linhof 617S II; Lens: Schneider 90mm; Filters: none; Medium: film, Fuji 120 Velvia 50 ISO; Shutter Speed: 1/4; Aperture: f22; Ratio: 3:1; Degrees: 87, shot on tripod; Image Size: 6cm x 17cm

Page 86 Cockpit Waterfall, Norfolk Island
Camera: Horseman SW-D II Pro body with P45+ back; Lens: 24mm; ISO: 50; Shutter Speed: 1 second; Aperture: f8; Exposure Compensation: 0.0; Resolution: 39MP

Page 87 Long Jetty, Central Coast, NSW
Camera: Phase One P645 body with P65+ back; Lens: 35mm; ISO: 50; Shutter Speed: 1/3; Aperture: f9; Exposure Compensation: –0.3; Resolution: 60.5MP

Page 88 Trailer Sailor, Morgan, SA
Camera: Horseman SW-D II Pro body with P65+ back; Lens: 23mm; ISO: 50; Shutter Speed: 1/60; Aperture: f11; Exposure Compensation: 0.0; Resolution: 60.5MP

Page 89 High Cliff, SA
Camera: Horseman SW-D II Pro body with P65+ back; Lens: 23mm; ISO: 50; Shutter Speed: 1/15; Aperture: f11; Exposure Compensation: 0.0; Resolution: 60.5MP

Pages 90–91 Kimberley Boabs, The Kimberley, WA
Camera: Linhof 617S II; Lens: Schneider 72mm; Filters: centre graduating filter; Medium: film, Fuji 220 Velvia 100 ISO; Shutter Speed: 8 seconds; Aperture: f22; Ratio: 3:1; Degrees: 100, shot on tripod; Image Size: 6cm x 17cm

Pages 92–93 Canal Rocks, WA
Camera: Phase One P645 body with P65+ back; Lens: 80mm; ISO: 50; Shutter Speed: 4 seconds; Aperture: f6.3; Exposure Compensation: 0.0; Resolution: 60.5MP, 15 image stitch

Pages 92–93 Whitehaven Beach, Whitsunday Island, Qld
Camera: Seitz Roundshot 220 VR; Lens: 55mm Pentax 67 with lens shift; Filters: none; Medium: film, Fuji 220 Velvia 50 ISO; Shutter Speed: 1/30; Aperture: f11.5; Ratio: 5:1; Degrees: 270 scan, shot on tripod; Image Size: 6cm x 30cm

Pages 94–95 Russell Falls, Mount Field National Park, Tas
Camera: Linhof 617S II; Lens: Schneider 90mm; Filters: 81B; Medium: film, Fuji 120 Velvia 100 ISO; Shutter Speed: 4–8 seconds; Aperture: f22; Ratio: 3:1; Degrees: 87, shot on tripod; Image Size: 6cm x 17cm

Page 96 Camels, Cable Beach, WA
Camera: Phase One P645 body with P65+ back; Lens: 35mm; ISO: 100; Shutter Speed: 1/200; Aperture: f4.5; Exposure Compensation: 0.0; Resolution: 60.5MP

Page 97 Palm Cove, Qld
Camera: Linhof 617S II; Lens: Schneider 72mm; Filters: centre graduating filter; Medium: film, Fuji 220 Velvia 100 ISO; Shutter Speed: 15 seconds; Aperture: f32; Ratio: 3:1; Degrees: 100, shot on tripod; Image Size: 6cm x 17cm

Page 97 Tread Lightly, Omeo, Vic
Camera: Linhof 617S II; Lens: Schneider 72mm; Filters: centre graduating filter; Medium: film, Fuji 220 Velvia 100 ISO; Shutter Speed: 1/2; Aperture: f32; Ratio: 3:1; Degrees: 100, shot on tripod; Image Size: 6cm x 17cm

Page 97 Secret Sanctuary, The Kimberley, WA
Camera: Linhof 617S II; Lens: Schneider 72mm; Filters: centre graduating filter; Medium: film, Fuji 220 Velvia 100 ISO; Shutter Speed: 2–4 seconds; Aperture: f32; Ratio: 3:1; Degrees: 100, shot on tripod; Image Size: 6cm x 17cm

Pages 98–100 Arkaba Woolshed, Flinders Ranges, SA
Camera: Phase One P645 body with P65+ back; Lens: 150mm; ISO: 100; Shutter speed: 1/5; Aperture: f16; Exposure Compensation: 0.0; Resolution: 60.5MP, 11 image stitch

Page 102 The Natural Bridge, Torndirrup National Park, WA
Camera: Horseman SW-D II Pro body with P65+ back; ISO: 50; Shutter Speed: 3 seconds; Aperture: f11; Exposure Compensation: 0.0; Resolution: 60.5MP

Page 103 Zenith Beach, Port Stephens, NSW
Camera: Horseman SW-D II Pro body with P65+ back; Lens:

23mm; ISO: 100; Shutter Speed: 1/2; Aperture: f11; Exposure Compensation: 0.0; Resolution: 60.5MP

Pages 104–105 Little Beach, Two Peoples Bay Nature Reserve, WA
Camera: Linhof 617S II; Lens: Schneider 72mm; Filters: centre graduating filter; Medium: film, Fuji 220 Velvia 100 ISO; Shutter Speed: 1 second; Aperture: f22; Ratio: 3:1; Degrees: 100, shot on tripod; Image Size: 6cm x 17cm

Pages 106–107 Tulips, Wynyard, Tas
Camera: Linhof 617S II; Lens: Schneider 90mm; Filters: none; Medium: film, Fuji 220 Velvia 50 ISO; Shutter Speed: 1/4; Aperture: f22.5; Ratio: 3:1; Degrees: 87, shot on tripod; Image Size: 6cm x 17cm

Page 108 Cephissus Creek, Cradle Mountain – Lake St Clair National Park, Tas
Camera: Linhof 617S II; Lens: Schneider 72mm; Filters: centre graduating filter & 81A filter; Medium: film, Fuji 120 Velvia 50 ISO; Shutter Speed: 8–15 seconds; Aperture: f22; Ratio: 3:1; Degrees: 100, shot on tripod; Image Size: 6cm x 17cm

Page 109 Cradle Mountain, Cradle Mountain – Lake St Clair National Park, Tas
Camera: Linhof 617S II; Lens: Schneider 72mm; Filters: centre graduating filter; Medium: film, Fuji 220 Velvia 50 ISO; Shutter Speed: 1/8; Aperture: f22; Ratio: 3:1; Degrees: 100, shot on tripod; Image Size: 6cm x 17cm

Page 110–111 Brumby Dawn, Benambra, Vic
Camera: Phase One P645 body with P65+ back; Lens: 80mm; ISO: 100; Shutter Speed: 8/10; Aperture: f10; Exposure Compensation: –0.3; Resolution: 60.5MP, 6 image stitch

Pages 112–113 Weeping Willow, Yarra Valley, Vic
Camera: Linhof 617S II; Lens: Schneider 90mm; Filters: none; Medium: film, Fuji 220 Velvia 100 ISO; Shutter Speed: 4 seconds; Aperture: f22; Ratio: 3:1; Degrees: 87, shot on tripod; Image Size: 6cm x 17cm

Pages 114–115 The Crossing, Swift's Creek, Vic
Camera: Linhof 617S II; Lens: Schneider 72mm; Filters: centre graduating filter; Medium: film, Fuji 220 Velvia 100 ISO; Shutter Speed: 1/4; Aperture: f22.5; Ratio: 3:1; Degrees: 100, shot on tripod; Image Size: 6cm x 17cm

Pages 116–117 MacKenzie Falls, The Grampians National Park, Vic
Camera: Phase One P645 body with P65+ back; Lens: 55mm; ISO: 50; Shutter Speed: 6/10; Aperture: f16; Exposure Compensation: 0.0; Resolution: 60.5MP, 9 image stitch

Pages 118–119 Mitchell Falls, The Kimberley, WA
Camera: Seitz Roundshot 220 VR; Lens: 75mm Pentax 67 with lens shift; Filters: none; Medium: film, Fuji 220 Velvia 50 ISO; Shutter Speed: 1/30; Aperture: f11.5; Ratio: 5:1; Degrees: 230 scan, shot on tripod; Image Size: 6cm x 30cm

Pages 120–122 Glycosmis Falls, The Kimberley, WA
Camera: Seitz Roundshot 220 VR; Lens: 75mm Pentax 67 with lens shift; Filters: none; Medium: film, Fuji 220 Velvia 50 ISO; Shutter Speed: 1/60; Aperture: f11; Ratio: 5:1; Degrees: 220 scan, shot on tripod; Image Size: 6cm x 30cm

Page 124 Mossman Mystique, Mossman, Qld
Camera: Linhof 617S II; Lens: Schneider 72mm; Filters: centre graduating filter; Medium: film, Fuji 220 Velvia 100 ISO; Shutter Speed: 1/2; Aperture: f22; Ratio: 3:1; Degrees: 100, shot on tripod; Image Size: 6cm x 17cm

Page 124 The Journey, Hill Inlet, Whitsunday Island, Qld
Camera: Linhof 617S II; Lens: Schneider 90mm; Filters: none; Medium: film, Fuji 220 Velvia 100 ISO; Shutter Speed: 1/250; Aperture: f11; Ratio: 3:1; Degrees: 87, handheld; Image Size: 6cm x 17cm

Page 124 Eagle Falls, The Kimberley, WA
Camera: Linhof 617S II; Lens: Schneider 72mm; Filters: centre graduating filter; Medium: film, Fuji 220 Velvia 100 ISO; Shutter Speed: 1/8; Aperture: f32; Ratio: 3:1; Degrees: 100, shot on tripod; Image Size: 6cm x 17cm

Page 125 Elabana Falls, Lamington National Park, Qld
Camera: Horseman SW-D II Pro body with P65+ back; Lens: 23mm; ISO: 50; Shutter Speed: 5 seconds; Aperture: f11; Exposure Compensation: 0.0; Resolution: 60.5MP

Page 126 Mawson's Hut (detail), Antarctica
Camera: Phase One P645 body with P45+ back; Lens: 80mm; ISO: 100; Shutter Speed: 1/285; Aperture: f8; Exposure Compensation: −0.7; Resolution: 39MP

Page 127 Whitsunday Aerial, Hill Inlet, Qld
Camera: Phase One P645 body with P45+ back; Lens: 80mm; ISO: 100; Shutter Speed: 1/800; Aperture: f9; Exposure Compensation: −0.3; Resolution: 39MP

Pages 128–129 Aerial, Whitsunday Island, Qld
Camera: Linhof 617S II; Lens: Schneider 72mm; Filters: centre graduating filter; Medium: film, Fuji 220 Velvia 100 ISO; Shutter Speed: 1/250; Aperture: f11; Ratio: 3:1; Degrees: 100, handheld; Image Size: 6cm x 17cm

Pages 130–131 Island Arch, Port Campbell National Park, Vic
Camera: Seitz Roundshot 220 VR; Lens: 75mm Pentax 67 with lens shift; Filters: none; Medium: film, Fuji 220 Velvia 100 ISO; Shutter Speed: 1 second; Aperture: f11; Ratio: 3:1; Degrees: 100 scan, shot on tripod; Image Size: 6cm x 17cm

Pages 130–131 Sunset, Eucla Dunes, WA
Camera: Seitz Roundshot 220 VR; Lens: 75mm Pentax 67 with lens shift; Filters: none; Medium: film, Fuji 220 Velvia 100 ISO; Shutter Speed: 1/2; Aperture: f11; Ratio: 5:1; Degrees: 230 scan, shot on tripod; Image Size: 6cm x 30cm

Page 132 Seven Mile Beach, Coffin Bay National Park, SA
Camera: Horseman SW-D II Pro body with P65+ back; Lens: 23mm; ISO: 50; Shutter Speed: 1 second; Aperture: f11; Exposure Compensation: 0.0; Resolution: 60.5MP

Page 133 Point Lowly Lighthouse, via Whyalla, SA
Camera: Horseman SW-D II Pro body with P65+ back; Lens: 23mm; ISO: 100; Shutter Speed: 9 seconds; Aperture: f11; Exposure Compensation: 0.0; Resolution: 60.5MP

Page 134 Aboriginal Kids, Arnhem Land, NT
Camera: Phase One P645 body with P65+ back; Lens: 35mm; ISO: 200; Shutter Speed: 1/320; Aperture: f4.5; Exposure Compensation: −0.3; Resolution: 60.5MP

Page 135 Sunset, Kata Tjuta, NT
Camera: Horseman SW-D II Pro body with P65+ back; Lens: 23mm; ISO: 50; Shutter Speed: 1/2; Aperture: f11; Exposure Compensation: 0.0; Resolution: 60.5MP

Pages 136–137 The Great Barrier Reef, Qld
Camera: Linhof 617S II; Lens: Schneider 90mm; Filters: none; Medium: film, Fuji 220 Velvia 100 ISO; Shutter Speed: 1/250; Aperture: f11; Ratio: 3:1; Degrees: 87; Image Size: 6cm x 17cm

Pages 138–140 Norah Head Lighthouse, NSW
Camera: Seitz Roundshot 220 VR; Lens: 75mm Pentax 67 with lens shift; Filters: none; Medium: film, Fuji 220 Velvia 100 ISO; Shutter Speed: 1/8; Aperture: f11; Ratio: 5:1; Degrees: 230 scan, shot on tripod; Image Size: 6cm x 30cm

Pages 142–143 Cradle Mountain from Kathleen's Pool, Tas
Camera: Linhof 617S II; Lens: Schneider 72mm; Filters: centre graduating filter; Medium: film, Fuji 220 Velvia 100 ISO; Shutter Speed: 1/8; Aperture: f22.5; Ratio: 3:1; Degrees: 100, shot on tripod; Image Size: 6cm x 17cm

Pages 144–145 King George Falls, The Kimberley, WA
Camera: Seitz Roundshot 220 VR; Lens: 75mm Pentax 67 with lens shift; Filters: none; Medium: film, Fuji 220 Velvia 50 ISO; Shutter Speed: 1/60; Aperture: f11.5; Ratio: 3:1; Degrees: 100 scan, shot on tripod; Image Size: 6cm x 17cm

Page 146 Piccaninny Creek, Purnululu National Park, WA
Camera: Phase One P645 body with P65+ back; Lens: 35mm; ISO: 50; Shutter Speed: 1/15; Aperture: f14; Exposure Compensation: 0.0; Resolution: 60.5MP

Page 147 Boab Tree, Fitzroy Crossing, WA
Camera: Phase One P645 body with P65+ back; Lens: 35mm; ISO: 100; Shutter Speed: 30 seconds; Aperture: f3.5; Exposure Compensation: 0.0; Resolution: 60.5MP

Page 148 Ragged Ranges, The Kimberley, WA
Camera: Panasonic Lumix DMC-LX2; Focal Length: 6.3; ISO: 100; Shutter Speed: 1/100; Aperture: f2.8; Exposure Compensation: −0.33; Resolution: 10MP

Page 149 Mertens Falls, The Kimberley, WA
Camera: Panasonic Lumix DMC-LX2; Lens: fixed lens; Focal Length: 6.3; ISO: 100; Shutter Speed: 1/400; Aperture: f5.6; Exposure Compensation: −0.33; Resolution: 10MP

Pages 150–151 Paradise, Fantome Island, Qld
Camera: Linhof 617S II; Lens: Schneider 90mm; Filters: none; Medium: film, Fuji 120 Velvia 50 ISO; Shutter Speed: 1/8; Aperture: f22.5; Ratio: 3:1; Degrees: 87, shot on tripod; Image Size: 6cm x 17cm

Pages 152–153 Sunrise, Main Beach, South West Rocks, NSW
Camera: Linhof 617S II; Lens: Schneider 72mm; Filters: centre graduating filter; Medium: film, Fuji 220 Velvia 100 ISO; Shutter Speed: 1/2; Aperture: f22; Ratio: 3:1; Degrees: 100, shot on tripod; Image Size: 6cm x 17cm

Pages 154–155 Sunrise, Emily Bay, Norfolk Island
Camera: Linhof 617S II; Lens: Schneider 72mm; Filters: centre graduating filter; Medium: film, Fuji 220 Velvia 100 ISO; Shutter Speed: 4– 8 seconds; Aperture: f22; Ratio: 3:1; Degrees: 100, shot on tripod; Image Size: 6cm x 17cm

Pages 156–158 Hill Inlet, Whitsunday Island, Qld
Camera: Seitz Roundshot 220 VR; Lens: 75mm Pentax 67 with lens shift; Filters: none; Medium: film, Fuji 220 Velvia 50 ISO; Shutter Speed: 1/60; Aperture: f16; Ratio: 5:1; Degrees: 230 scan, shot on tripod; Image Size: 6cm x 30cm

Index of Images

About the Photographer

Ken Duncan strives for the highest excellence in everything he does. His artworks are owned by members of royalty and national rulers; by movie stars and music industry icons; by business leaders, investors, collectors and private individuals all over the world.

Well known as the pioneer of panoramic photography in Australia, Ken was one of the first to promote photography as an art form in Australia. In 2006 he was granted an Honorary Fellowship from the Australian Institute of Professional Photography in recognition of his outstanding contribution to the industry. In 2009, Ken was presented with a Medal of the Order of Australia (OAM) for his services to landscape photography, publishing and the arts. He was also the recipient of the photographic industry's highest honour — the PICA Gold Tripod award.

Since establishing his own publishing company in 1992, Ken has published in excess of fifty individual photographic books, the majority of which continue to reprint year after year. He is also a popular speaker and has developed a range of spectacular audio-visual presentations.

Ken Duncan has been described by *A Current Affair* as "definitely one of Australia's most iconic image makers". A leading American gallery dubbed him "the Ansel Adams of colour photography". *Australian Professional Photography* magazine described him as "undoubtedly Australia's (and possibly the world's) leading exponent of panoramic landscape photography". In addition, Ken was chosen by Mel Gibson to shoot on the set of his epic movie *The Passion of the Christ*.

Despite hundreds of outstanding commentaries on his work, in his own words Ken is simply "an average photographer with a great God". There is no doubt God has given him a great gift to capture and present the splendour of creation.

AUSTRALIA – OUR ISLAND PARADISE
First published 2011 and reprinted 2012
by Panographs Publishing Pty Ltd
ABN 21 050 235 606
PO Box 3015, Wamberal,
NSW, 2260, Australia
Telephone +61 2 4367 6777
Email: panos@kenduncan.com

Photography & text by Ken Duncan
©2011 Divine Guidance P/L
Designed by John Bull, Publishing Art Australia
Reprographics by CFL Print Studio, www.createdforlife.com
Printed in China by Everbest Printing Co. Ltd

The National Library of Australia
Cataloguing-in-Publication entry
Author: Duncan, Ken
Title: Australia : our island paradise / Ken Duncan
ISBN: 9780980834314 (hbk.)
Notes: Includes index
Subjects: Landscape photography-Australia
Photography, Panoramic-Australia
Australia-Pictorial works
Dewey Number: 778.360994

To view Ken Duncan Limited Edition Prints, visit:
• 414 The Entrance Road, Erina Heights, NSW
Telephone +61 2 4367 6701
• 73 George Street, The Rocks, Sydney, NSW
Telephone +61 2 9241 3460
• Level 1, 9 Star Circus, Harbour Town Shopping Centre, Docklands, Vic
Telephone +61 3 9670 6971

www.kenduncan.com